A Gift for

_____

From

_____

Date

_____

Whisper a Prayer for Moms

Copyright © 2004 by Mark Gilroy Communications, Inc.

Designed by Beth Sparkman

Photography credits:
Pages: 6, 8, 12, 14, 16, 18, 24, 26, 28, 30, 32, 38, 42, 44, 48, 52, 54, 56, 62, 64, 66, 68, 75, 78-80 © by Photos.com; Pages: 20, 82 © by Images State; Pages: 10, 84, 88-90 © by Alamy; Pages: 4, 94 © by Photodisc; Pages: 22, 36, 50, 76 © by Michael Hudson; Pages: cover, title page, 40, 46, 70, 74 © by Digital Vision; Pages: 60, 71-72, 86 © by Brand X; Page: 58 © by Corbis. All rights reserved.

ISBN 0-8423-3481-5

Printed in the United States of America

09 08 07 06 05 04
6 5 4 3 2 1

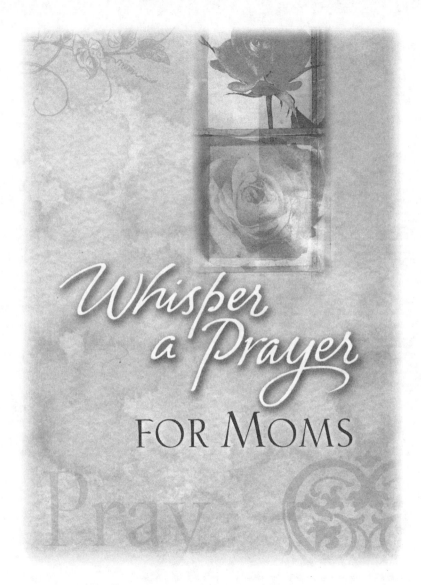

Whisper
a Prayer

FOR MOMS

TYNDALE HOUSE PUBLISHERS, INC.
WHEATON, ILLINOIS

Don't worry about anything; instead, pray about everything. Tell God what you need, and thank him for all he has done. If you do this, you will experience God's peace, which is far more wonderful than the human mind can understand.

Philippians 4:6-7, NLT

Introduction: Experience God's Peace

Are you looking for counsel on a tough decision ?

Do you feel an incredible sense of gratitude for the many ways that God has blessed your life?

Are you worried about a particular circumstance in your life?

Do you sense the need for a special touch of God's protection for your family? for your children?

Whether you are alone or in a crowd, whether your need seems great or small, God invites you to bring all your worries, all your needs, all your worship...all your life before him. He will hear the faintest whisper.

Whisper a Prayer for Moms presents thought-provoking and heartfelt prayers to help you express to God your cares and joys as a mother.

Are you ready to experience God's wonderful peace? Simply whisper a prayer.

Always keep yourselves united in the Holy Spirit, and bind yourselves together with peace.

Ephesians 4:3, NLT

Unity for My Family

Dear Heavenly Father,

Thank you for my family. I am so blessed and feel so much gratitude for all you have given me. I ask that you help my family to be united through the presence of the Holy Spirit in our home. Plant a love for one another in our hearts that will overcome any difficult days ahead.

I know some families that are in strife and some that are now separated. You know the families on my heart. I pray that their anger and bitterness will be replaced by love, compassion, and forgiveness.

Thank you for helping me to become a mother who provides her family with a sense of security and peace.

Let us stop just saying we love each other; let
us really show it by our actions. It is by our
actions that we know we are living in the truth.

1 John 3:18-19, NLT

Living the Truth

O Mighty God,

You have shown us what true love is by sending your Son to die for our sins. We can never repay the price you paid for our redemption.

By my actions, I want to teach my family what true love is. Help me to model patience, kindness, sacrifice, and other expressions of godliness in my words and especially in my deeds.

Thank you for forgiving me when I have failed. I am so grateful that even as I watch my child grow up, you are raising me to reach maturity in my faith and life.

If God cares so wonderfully for flowers that are here today and gone tomorrow, won't he more surely care for you? . . . Your heavenly Father already knows all your needs, and he will give you all you need from day to day if you live for him.

Matthew 6:30, 32-33, NLT

You Know What I Need

Dear Heavenly Father,

I get so caught up in my needs and problems that I sometimes forget that you are the giver of all good gifts and that you meet all my needs.

You have assured me that I don't have to live in fear and stress, but I simply need to trust you. So right now I bring my financial concerns and all other worries and needs to you.

I know that I don't have all the answers, but I choose to live with confidence and faith because you promise to give me exactly what I need each day.

Teach your children to choose the right path,
and when they are older, they will remain
upon it.

Proverbs 22:6, NLT

Teaching My Children

Gentle Shepherd,

Since I accepted you into my heart, you have taught me so much about right and wrong, about the things that are important in life, about living a life of integrity and peace and joy.

I ask that you send many great teachers into my children's lives. I also pray that you make me into a teacher who instills wisdom into their minds and hearts, so that they will make right decisions now—and for a lifetime. Help me to be a model of God's patience, love, and compassion so my children can learn through me.

I know that the Holy Spirit is the greatest teacher and that he will help me overcome my shortcomings as I do the best I can.

Do not forget to do good and to share with
others, for with such sacrifices God is pleased.

Hebrews 13:16, NIV

Pleasing God

Merciful God,

You are an awesome God, full of compassion and kindness. Your love and mercy know no bounds. Your heart is always turned toward those who are hurting and those who have serious needs.

I want to do good deeds and help others. I know that my family needs me. But I also know how much it pleases you when I reach out to others. I ask that you renew in me a heart of compassion and give me the strength to do something about it.

As I share with the needy, I will also remember to praise you for the many blessings you have given me.

Are you tired? Worn out? Burned out on
religion? Come to me. Get away with me and
you'll recover your life. I'll show you how to
take a real rest. Walk with me and work with
me—watch how I do it.

Matthew 11:28-29, *THE MESSAGE*

Rest for My Soul

O Lord,

I come to you with a sense of weariness. I'm not sure
how I can get everything done. I don't feel like I have
anything left to offer.

Thank you for inviting me to bring my burdens
to you. Thank you for having the empathy to know
that sometimes I get tired and I struggle to express
faith and hope positively. I am so humbled that you
still accept and embrace me as I am and that you offer
to carry my load with me.

O Lord, just knowing that you are close to me
right now gives rest to my soul.

God is not a God of disorder but of peace.

1 Corinthians 14:33, NLT

My Life Is Cluttered!

Dear God,

My life is cluttered right now. My household is not in order. I can't find anything. We are running too many different directions. I'm forgetting things and then showing up late!

I know, dear God, that you are not the author of confusion. I know that the enemy of my soul would love to create so many distractions and worries that I forget to trust you. He would love nothing more than to rob me of my joy.

But you are a God of peace. I turn to you right now for guidance. I know that as I lean on you today, you will bring a new sense of order and peace to my life and to my household. Thank you for peace.

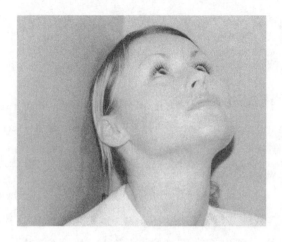

Be strong and courageous. Do not be afraid or terrified because of them, for the Lord your God goes with you; he will never leave you nor forsake you.

Deuteronomy 31:6, NIV

Courage

O Lord My God,

With you on my side, I know that I have absolutely nothing to fear. Still, at times, I take my eyes off you and begin to lose heart.

You know the neglected areas of my life where I need to stretch and grow. You know the challenges I need to own up to and face. You know the uncertainty I feel about the future.

It is so comforting to know that you go ahead of me and lead the way. Thank you for the courage to face the challenges and the future that lie ahead of me.

The Lord is my shepherd, I shall not be in want.

He makes me lie down in green pastures,

he leads me beside quiet waters,

he restores my soul.

Psalm 23:1-2, NIV

My Shepherd

Heavenly Father,

It is so wonderful to stop each day to spend time alone with you in prayer and in your Word. You are such a good shepherd, who knows when I need rest, when I need to pull away from the noises of life to experience peace and quiet.

My Shepherd, please help me to make time in my day to spend with you. Remind me that the deepest need of my life is not any material possession I don't have, but to be close to you—for then everything else takes care of itself.

Thank you for green pastures and quiet waters.

How great is the love the Father has lavished on

us, that we should be called the children of God!

1 John 3:1, NIV

Your Child

Abba Father,

When I look at my children, my heart is filled with wonder. Even when I get impatient, irritable, or angry, I still feel so humbled to be a mother, to have someone to love this much.

I am amazed that you feel the same way—and so much more—about me. I am unbelievably honored that you call me your child, that you are a true Father to me.

Today I have a bounce in my step and a smile on my face, knowing what a wonderful Father you are!

In everything set them an example by doing what is good. In your teaching show integrity, seriousness and soundness of speech that cannot be condemned.

Titus 2:7-8, NIV

Integrity

Dear Lord,

I know that I'm not perfect and that I won't always say and do the right thing with my children. Help me to have the courage and grace to say I'm sorry when needed.

Even if I'm not perfect, I want to be known as a person of integrity and strong character. When my children look at my life, I want them to understand that a relationship with you creates a life of integrity.

Dear Lord, I want my children to be proud of me, but most of all, I want you to be proud of the person I've become since I met you.

Discipline your children, and they will give

you happiness and peace of mind.

Proverbs 29:17, NLT

Help Me to Be Firm

Gracious God,

You know when I struggle to discipline my children. Sometimes it is easier to ignore bad behavior than to correct it. Sometimes I am more caught up in preserving my children's happiness than in building their character. Sometimes I even worry about what my children will think of me when I say no.

I know that just as you love me enough to correct me, I show greater love for my children when I discipline them. So I ask you for discernment to know which attitudes and actions need correction. I ask for poise so that my discipline will never be characterized by anger and harshness. I ask for consistency so that my children will know what is expected of them.

Gracious God, with gratitude I receive the happiness and peace you promise.

I am my beloved's,

and his desire is toward me.

Song of Solomon 7:10, NKJV

My Beloved

Loving Savior,

Thank you for the gift of romance. Let me paint a beautiful picture of love for my children by the love I show their father. Help me to joyfully model affection, respect, and kindness in my words and actions.

For every mother who is single, I pray that you would be the husband she is without and the everyday father her children need. For every mother who has married again, I pray that you will supernaturally create a family filled with a spirit of gratitude, unity, love, and forgiveness. For every mom in a troubled relationship, I pray that you would grant her a peace that can only come from you.

I am grateful that, beyond any human affection, you are my beloved God.

Give thanks to the Lord, for he is good;

his love endures forever.

Psalm 107:1, NIV

thank you, Lord

Thank You

Dear Lord,

Because of your Spirit within me, I am a person of gratitude! I refuse to take my blessing of family for granted. I refuse to complain about petty annoyances and inconveniences. I refuse to focus on what I don't have when I live in a land of plenty. I refuse to grumble and gossip when there is so much positive to see and say.

Today, Lord, I say thank you, thank you, thank you, thank you! And I'm not going to stop there. I plan to tell others how grateful I am for your goodness and your love that endures forever.

Even as I say thank you, I receive so much in return as my soul is renewed and my whole outlook on life is lifted.

Peace I leave with you; My peace I give to you; not as the world gives, do I give to you.

John 14:27, NASB

A Divine Peace

Dear God of All Peace,

There are areas of my life that don't feel very peaceful right now. I know it is because I have looked to the media for images of success and fulfillment, or I have asked loved ones to provide a level of contentment that they don't have the power to grant. Sometimes I have even depended on my children to make me happy.

You have sent your Son, Jesus, as the one way to peace in our world—and in my life. He alone provides a peace that doesn't depend on what is happening around me. I thank you so much that when I put my focus back on Jesus, peace always follows.

Dear God, your gifts truly are the best.

Be silent, and know that I am God!

Psalm 46:10, NLT

Be Silent

Dear God,

When I am in your presence, there are no awkward pauses. I am not judged by whether I have all the right words to say. Your Spirit speaks on my behalf when I can't express my thoughts as clearly as I would like.

And just as you invite me to voice all my worries and needs to you, you bid me to come silently before you, so that I can realize again how awesome you are; so that I can hear your voice as you speak to me with encouragement, direction, and correction; so that I can feel the spiritual intimacy of just being close to you.

I will praise you audibly with my lips—and silently with my heart.

I AM GOD

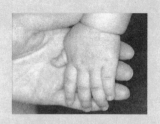

What is faith? It is the confident assurance that what we hope for is going to happen. It is the evidence of things we cannot yet see. God gave his approval to people in days of old because of their faith. By faith we understand that the entire universe was formed at God's command, that what we now see did not come from anything that can be seen.

Hebrews 11:1-3, NLT

Confident Assurance

Faithful God,

I have so many hopes and dreams for my children. But you know that I also have questions and natural worries. Will they be successful and happy? Will they be persons of integrity? Will they know you and love you and serve you?

Right now I place my children in your hands. I may not be able to see the future, but I have the confident assurance that your dreams for them are bigger than mine, that you are going to work in them and through them.

You have miraculously created a magnificent world. I thank you most of all for the miracle of my children.

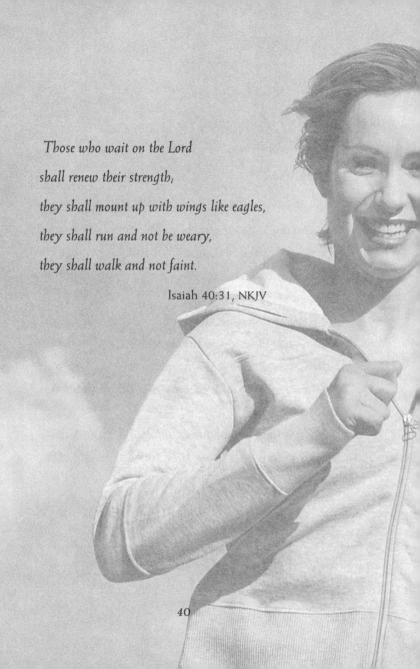

Those who wait on the Lord

shall renew their strength;

they shall mount up with wings like eagles,

they shall run and not be weary,

they shall walk and not faint.

Isaiah 40:31, NKJV

40

Soaring

O Mighty Lord,

I ask that you give me a renewed strength, vision, optimism, joyfulness, determination, courage, sense of humor, confidence, love, kindness, compassion, playfulness, faith, friendliness, gentleness, patience, and all the other dynamics that will make me a light in the world.

Even though I have come to you feeling weary, O Lord, just talking to you, spending time with you, and waiting before you give me a sense of hope, a feeling that I can soar.

Thank you for teaching me to fly!

He is their shield, protecting those who walk
with integrity. He guards the paths of justice
and protects those who are faithful to him.

Proverbs 2:7-8, NLT

Protect Us

Dear Lord,

I ask that you protect my family today. I know there is an evil one who is committed to destroying families, undermining the love between husbands and wives, and disrupting the relationship between parents and children. I know many people have fallen under Satan's influence and do his dirty work for him.

On behalf of my family, I express my faith with complete confidence today. I know you will guard our paths. I am certain you will protect us from all forms of harm, whether it be physical danger or spiritual temptation.

Lord, you are my family's shield.

God blesses the people who patiently endure
testing. Afterward they will receive the crown
of life that God has promised to those who
love him.

James 1:12, NLT

Trials

My God,

You know how much I want to avoid trials in my life—and how much I want to shield my children from trials.

But I know that my growth and happiness are not based on everything going my way, but are in large measure the result of how I handle adversity. Renew my confidence that you are blessing me, even in the tough times.

I also ask that you help me believe in my children enough to not step in and rescue them from every test they face, knowing that you are blessing them in the same way.

There are "friends" who destroy each other,

but a real friend sticks closer than a brother.

Proverbs 18:24, NLT

My Friends

Dear God,

I pray for my friend who is angry; please help her to forgive those who have wronged her.

I pray for my friend who is hurt; please help her to receive the comfort she so desperately craves.

I pray for my friend who has hurt me; please help me to extend the same mercy and forgiveness that you give so freely to me.

I pray for my friend who is struggling with temptation; please help me to offer spiritual support. If she is not open to counsel, help me to have the wisdom to know when to back away.

I pray for my friend who has taught me so much about your goodness and love; please help me to return that encouragement to her and others.

I will praise You, O Lord my God, with all
my heart,
and I will glorify Your name forevermore.
For great is Your mercy toward me.

Psalm 86:12-13, NKJV

Glory to Your Name

O Lord My God,

I have so many reasons to praise you—most of all for your great love, which is flowing in my heart right now.

Today I will boldly and joyfully tell my family, my friends, and my neighbors how great you are. I am going to worship you when I am in the car, when I am at the store, when I am eating a meal, when I am doing chores, when I read my child a story tonight, when I lie down in bed at the end of the day.

I will not take your name in vain, O Lord my God. I will only give you the glory you so richly deserve.

The eternal God is your refuge,

and his everlasting arms are under you.

Deuteronomy 33:27, NLT

A Safe Haven

Eternal God,

Truly you are my refuge when I feel threatened because there are evil people in the world who would harm my family if they had opportunity.

Rather than live in fear, I take comfort and gain confidence in the knowledge that you wrap your arms of love and protection around me and my family.

Make us wise, O God, so that we will do our part to carefully avoid dangerous situations. Thank you for the times you have protected us when we didn't even know we were in danger, and for the times you will protect us in the future.

O Lord, you are so good, so ready to forgive,
so full of unfailing love for all who ask your aid.

Psalm 86:5, NLT

Unfailing Love

Dear Lord,

So many times we don't receive what we need from you because we fail to ask for your help. But you invite us to bring every care and concern we have and come boldly before you.

Today I ask for your help for a relationship problem you already know about, for a situation that needs your intervention concerning my child, for the grace and strength to forgive others just as you have forgiven me.

You are a good God. Help me to express that same forgiveness and love to the people in my life.

O Lord, you alone are my hope.

I've trusted you, O Lord, from childhood.

Psalm 71:5, NLT

Expectations

Dear Lord,

I pray that I will never lose my childlike faith, hopes, and dreams. I don't want my expectations to be quashed by disappointments. I don't want life's hardships to rob me of my sense of the great things you have in store for me.

Lord, will you remind me of the dreams and hopes you planted in my heart from childhood? Will you fan into a mighty flame the mere spark of faith that I know I have right now?

Lord, it is wonderful to serve a God who believes in me so much that you even entrust dreams to me!

Above all things have fervent love for one another,

for "love will cover a multitude of sins."

1 Peter 4:8, NKJV

love

Love One Another

Gracious God,

My life is different today. I will not criticize my family. I refuse to dwell on negative thoughts toward my friends, my country's leaders, or others whom I randomly encounter—even bad drivers.

Your amazing grace toward me has inspired me to pass that love on to my children. You have said that there is nothing greater than love, and I truly feel that right now. How wonderful to believe in my children as you do.

God, when I am tempted to fall back into old patterns of judgmentalism, I ask that you stir the flame of fervent love in my heart again.

He heals the brokenhearted

and binds up their wounds.

Psalm 147:3, NIV

The Brokenhearted

Dear God,

I lift before you a number of people who are broken-hearted . . .

- ◆ a special friend who has lost a spouse,
- ◆ my child's friend whose family is enmeshed in strife and chaos,
- ◆ a person from my church who is suffering from a terrible physical condition,
- ◆ a neighbor who has lost his job and is facing financial difficulties.

You are a friend to the needy, including me. I pray that these hurting people you have placed on my heart would receive from you an incredible sense of comfort and healing.

Don't worry about anything; instead, pray about everything. Tell God what you need, and thank him for all he has done. If you do this, you will experience God's peace, which is far more wonderful than the human mind can understand.

Philippians 4:6-7, NLT

No Worries?

Dear God,

When you tell me not to worry, I am tempted to laugh, because worry comes so easily to me. (And I'm not the only one.)

You invite me to pray about everything, tell you exactly what I need, and thank you for all you have done for me already and for all you are going to do in the days ahead.

It's not easy and it doesn't come naturally, but today I set aside worry—about my children, about finances, about needs among my friends—and I thank you right now for your peace, which is far more wonderful than my mind can understand.

The Lord says, "I will guide you along
the best pathway for your life.
I will advise you and watch over you."

Psalm 32:8, NLT

What Should I Do?

Lord,

You know that I want to please you, to serve you, to follow your will for my life. But sometimes I don't know how best to do that.

Lord, I need your counsel. I know there are many good activities I could pursue, many excellent paths I could follow. But would you show me the *best* path for my life? I don't want to look back on my life with regret because I didn't accomplish what you most wanted me to do.

I cling to your promise that you will guide me and watch over my life. I know you are quietly speaking to me even now. Help me to shut out the distractions, to be open and receptive, as I listen for your voice today.

Hold to the truth in love.

Ephesians 4:15, NLT

Honest Love

Dear Heavenly Father,

I pray that you would teach me to speak to my children with words that are both honest and loving. You know the times when I have been honest but harsh. You know the times when I have been loving but false.

I thank you that as my loving heavenly Father you speak to me with truth and love. I know that I'm far from perfect, but because of your Son, Jesus Christ, I know that I can accomplish things that aren't possible in my own strength and wisdom.

Following your ways leads to peace, my Father. Today I will walk in peace through my words of love and truth.

We can make our plans, but the Lord
determines our steps.

Proverbs 16:9, NLT

My Plans

O Lord,

You want me to use my brains to make the best decisions in life for my family. You give me the wisdom and energy to plan ahead.

I gain incredible confidence from the fact that, after I've done the very best I can as a mother and as your child, you truly guard and guide my steps. There have been so many times when things didn't turn out the way I planned, but through you, they turned out even better.

I'll keep doing the best I can—and trusting you with all my heart.

abundance

You have given me greater joy

than those who have abundant harvests

of grain and wine.

Psalm 4:7, NLT

blessed my life

Abundance of the Heart

O God,

I have enjoyed such an abundant harvest in my life.
I can scarcely ask for more, because you've already
given me so much. A warm home. A family. Good
food. And many other blessings.

But my greatest joys are not in a harvest of
material possessions or grand accomplishments. My
deepest joy is found in the wonderful experiences
that are mine as a mother, as a wife, as your child.

No wonder you tell us in your Word to remember your mighty deeds and the ways that you have
worked on our behalf. I won't forget the ways your
presence has blessed my life, and I will continue to
thank you for the simple memories that last a lifetime.

thank you

"I was hungry and you fed me, I was thirsty and you gave me a drink, I was homeless and you gave me a room, I was shivering and you gave me clothes, I was sick and you stopped to visit, I was in prison and you came to me."

… Then the King will say, "I'm telling the solemn truth: Whenever you did one of these things to someone overlooked or ignored, that was me—you did it to me."

Matthew 25:34, 36, *THE MESSAGE*

Eyes of Compassion

O God My King,

When I think of the number of children who are overlooked and ignored, my heart is broken. I can hardly stand the thought that there are children who are homeless, who go to bed hungry, who are sick but receive no medical care, who are imprisoned in circumstances where there is no love.

May I never take my own children for granted. Give me eyes of compassion to the needy around me. Help me to have enough love to act on my compassion—and to teach my children the joy of giving to others.

May I realize that whatever small blessing I provide for someone in need I am doing it for Jesus.

Through the Lord's mercies we are not consumed,

because His compassions fail not.

They are new every morning;

great is Your faithfulness.

Lamentations 3:22-23, NKJV

New Each Day

Merciful Lord,

You promise to give my family new mercies every single morning of our lives. We don't have to carry over grace, mercy, or faith from yesterday. Your fresh touch is up-to-date every day.

Father, I receive your mercies today with a deep sense of gratitude and appreciation—knowing full well how much I need them. And whether my days are tough or easy, I don't want to ever take this gift from you lightly or for granted.

I will rejoice and give you praise, O Lord, for the tender mercies that are mine for knowing and trusting you.

*A gentle answer turns away wrath, but harsh
words stir up anger. . . . Gentle words bring
life and health.*

Proverbs 15:1, 4, NLT

wise and

Gentle Words

Dear God,

When I think of the times I have not controlled my tongue, when I have lashed out in anger at my family, I am truly embarrassed and sorry. I know that harsh words only stir up more anger. Please forgive me.

I pray that I will speak words that bring life and health to my husband, to my children, to my close friends—even to casual acquaintances. I want my speech to be wise and filled with grace.

Through your words my life has been changed forever. I pray that, in some small way, my words will bless the ones I love so much.

filled with grace

My flesh and my heart fail;
but God is the strength of my heart
and my portion forever.

Psalm 73:26, NKJV

I Don't Feel Adequate

Dear God,

You have promised not to allow burdens to come my way without also providing me the strength to handle them.

But I confess that there are times when I haven't been strong enough to triumph over the circumstances I have faced. I've not exhibited the poise and grace that should characterize my life. And when I look at other mothers who seem to have it all together, my sense of inadequacy is heightened.

What amazes me is that when I confess my lack of personal power, you step in to do for me what I cannot do myself. I am humbled by the realization that you are my true source of strength. I am adequate—not because of my own ability but because you make me more than adequate for my tasks.

A cheerful heart is good medicine.

Proverbs 17:22, NLT

laugh

smile

Laughter

Wise God,

Thank you for creating laughter to brighten our lives. There are times for being somber, respectful, and appropriately serious, but you also invite us to cut loose, to celebrate, smile, and laugh at the humor and levity of life.

Today I remember that you are God—and you have the world under control. I'm not going to worry, judge, or walk around with a scowl on my face. I'm going to enjoy the sound of my children's laughter. I'm going to be an example of a joyful, thankful child of the King.

celebrate

Be kind to each other, tenderhearted,

forgiving one another, just as God

through Christ has forgiven you.

Ephesians 4:32, NLT

Forgiveness

Dear God,

You reached out to me in kindness before I ever acknowledged you. You offered me forgiveness for my sins before I was even willing to admit I'm a sinner. You loved me when my attitudes and actions made me very unlovable. Thank you for the way you treated me with such tenderness. Thank you for not giving up on me when I was too stubborn to change.

And thank you that you offer me the same opportunity to be kind, tender, patient, loving, and forgiving to others, especially to my children.

When I think of the incredible sacrifice of Jesus Christ, I won't complain when others aren't responsive, but I'll be thankful once again for what you've done for me.

Let us not grow weary while doing good,
for in due season we shall reap if we do not
lose heart.

Galatians 6:9, NKJV

I Won't Give Up

Dear Lord,

Even if my friends forsake me… I won't give up.

Even if my children go through a period of rebellion … I won't give up.

Even if my husband and I struggle for a season … I won't give up.

Even if my church experiences problems and strife … I won't give up.

Even if my life doesn't measure up to what you expect from me and what I expect from myself … I won't give up.

You have helped me to plant seeds of faith and grace through my good deeds. And you have promised that if I persist, if I don't give up, there will be a great harvest in the right season.

Lord, great days are ahead. I won't give up!

Whatever your hand finds to do,

do it with all your might.

Ecclesiastes 9:10, NIV

With All My Might

Mighty God,

You know that in our society it is not always very prestigious to be a mother. Sometimes the attention and adulation seem to flow unfairly toward the very young or the singularly career minded who don't have children.

I know how easy it is to be overly sensitive and feel slighted. And I know that motherhood is a great honor. More importantly, I know in my heart that I wouldn't have it any other way.

I pray right now that you will renew my passion for being someone called Mommy. What a privilege! What a joy! I want to raise my children with all my might!

Let us lay aside every weight, and the sin
which so easily ensnares us, and let us run
with endurance the race that is set before us.

Hebrews 12:1, NKJV

The Race

Gracious Father,

A relationship with you is not like a hundred-meter sprint—one quick burst and it's finished. Rather, you desire a relationship with me that is like a marathon, covering every day of my life.

You know the unhealthy baggage I have allowed to accumulate in my life, slowing my pace and causing me to stumble. I ask that you grant me the resolve and the grace to rid myself of habits and attitudes that keep me from fully serving and loving you and my family.

Thank you, gracious Father, that you await me at the ultimate finish line with an embrace and a crown that will last forever.

As a mother comforts

her child, so will

I comfort you.

Isaiah 66:13, NIV

As a Mother

Heavenly Father,

I can't imagine a greater love than the love a mother has for her children—the love that I have for *my* children. No wonder they look first to me for comfort when they are hurt.

Father, your infinite loving-kindness is far beyond the finite love I can give to my children. Your comfort reaches all the way to the depths of my soul, reviving my spirit.

Whenever I feel that I am giving more than I am receiving in life, I will remember the everlasting love you lavish on me. You are my Father, God. Yet you love me as tenderly as a mother.

I myself have gained much joy and comfort

from your love.

Philemon 1:7, NLT

Help for the Journey

Dear God,

I am so grateful for the wonderful people you have brought across my path to help me on my journey as a follower of Jesus Christ. I have received great counsel and comfort. I have been challenged and encouraged. Prayers have come before your throne because of the love these friends have for me.

I am so happy that the Christian walk is not a solitary trek. I am awed by the reality that when I grow closer to you, I grow closer to others, to my friends, and to my family.

You alone are perfect, and only you are absolutely trustworthy. Thank you that you have enriched my life so much with people who are like angels to me.

Never let loyalty and kindness get away from you! Wear them like a necklace; write them deep within your heart. Then you will find favor with both God and people, and you will gain a good reputation.

Proverbs 3:3-4, NLT

A Good Reputation

Heavenly Father,

When I am loyal and kind, I attain favor from the people in my life, and most of all, from you. Guard my reputation so that it brings glory to your name.

I confess that at times I have coveted the high regard of others, but I want it without the inconvenience of extending myself through loyalty and kindness. I know there are no shortcuts to a good reputation.

I pray that my primary motive would be to please you by being a blessing to others. Even something as valuable as a good reputation is secondary to my relationship with you.

I am sure that God, who began the good work within you, will continue his work until it is finally finished on that day when Christ Jesus comes back again.

Philippians 1:6, NLT

Not Finished Yet—
But Someday

Dear God,

I am growing in my faith. I am growing in my knowledge of your Word. I am growing as a woman and as a mother. I am growing in my ministry to others. Sometimes I fall short in my attitudes and actions. Still, I'm growing.

What a wonderful work you began in my life. You gave me peace, confidence, and gentleness I never knew before.

On my final day on earth, dear God, whether it is because Jesus comes back to gather those who love him or because I am at the moment of my death, I look forward to seeing you face-to-face and knowing that your work in my life has been perfected.

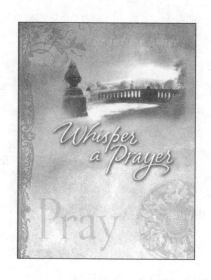 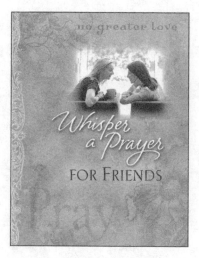

Also from Tyndale House Publishers

Whisper a Prayer (0-8423-8293-3)

Whisper a Prayer for Friends (0-8423-8296-8)

Available at your favorite local retailer.